Notes on…Love and Hate

~~~

Works by Jordan Merritt

Short Fiction

The Music Box

Novel

Thin Atoms

Notes on…Love and Hate

a collection of poetry

by

Jordan Merritt

Notes on…Love and Hate

Copyright © 2024 by Jordan Merritt

All rights reserved.

This poetry collection is protected under the copyright laws of the United States of America. Any reproduction or unauthorized use of the material herein is prohibited without the express written permission of the author.

To all of the women I ever loved.

Table of Contents

"Lonely Road" 1
"Goodnight" 2
"The Girl on the Slope" 3
"Angel" 4
"Loving" 5
"Azure" 6
"Electricity" 7
"Object" 8
"Remnant" 9
"Enraptured" 10
"Rhythmic Echoes" 11
"Masterpiece" 12
"Incident" 13
"The Wilderness Within" 14
"Prodigal Son" 15
"Cherubesque" 16
"Sunlit Devotion" 18
"Eternal Embrace" 19
"Echoes of Blue" 20
"Hollow Dissonance" 22
"Soul Attention" 24
"Full Circle" 25
"Tempest of the Murky Waters" 26
"Portrait of Ambition" 29
"Symphony of the Night" 30
"An Anatomical Quest" 31
"The Radiant Apology" 32
"Simpatico Reverie" 33
"Nothing in Between" 34
"Whispers in the Clouds" 36
"Soundly Sleeping" 38
"At a Loss" 39

"The Bearing of Historical Weight" 41
"Love's Dignitary" 42
"The Essence of a Whisper" 43
"My Painted Lady" 45
"My Painted Lady: Redux" 47
"Dance of Uncertainty" 49

"Lonely Road"

It was indeed my face you saw
on that long and lonesome road,
but it never was my intention
to make your heart grow cold.

I would never ask you to lose control
or tear down your walls, brick by brick.

Never would I lead you astray
or ask you to do things that you do not wish,
but your absence is like a desert,
and I am a dying fish.

All I want is, exclusively, you, and that want,
I will not deter,
for you look so peaceful when you sleep.
Oh, how gently you stir.

I love it more when you are awake,
gazing deep into my soul.
You are the puzzle piece that makes me,
once again, feel whole.

I know your heart is strong and
will always find the way,
but let me make this road not lonely.
Let me be with you.

Let me stay.

"Goodnight"

There is no one in sight.
There is no one near nor far.
All the white celestial moon light
hides behind the stars.

The break of dawn
with the people gone,
it is only you and me.
The houses bare,
the glass is bent
refracting what I see.

Everyone else is still at rest,
but you, my love,
are by far the best.

My love for you is in the stars
above this ethereal city,
so come away with me instead
my beautiful, heavenly pretty.

"The Girl on the Slope"

On the side of a slope, an angel revolving.
Her dress of Heaven,
in fields of sapphires and diamonds.

Flames disperse through of her movements,
by all dreams and every joy
and the comforts of euphoria
string out through her curvatures.

Behind her beauty is the Orient line of elation.

And while this goddess in the distance
is made of the pulsating sound of my love-struck heart,
the flowery softness of her touch
and all her being flows over the side of the slope
like a basket of emotion poured onto my mind
and turns my abyss beneath me a
flowering blue.

"Angel"

When I saw her, my mind set fire.

To see her sit there, calmly reading,

and my eyes follow as she is leaving.

There is no pain that is proceeding.

I would renounce myself to see her breathing.

And when I see her,

I imagine she loved her heavenly wings

before she fell to Earth,

but if she had not lost them,

I would not have fallen for her first.

"Loving"

She puts her face into mine,
liquor on her breath.

She asked me for the time,
and then I took her to her bed.

She rocked me all night
and all throughout the day.

Her loving feels so right
that yes is all I can say.

"Azure"

When I look for treasure,
I open azure.

She is sitting there,
far more beautiful than
perfection could ever be.

Her outstanding complexion
shines against a pale moon's light.
She fulfills me like no other.

I see my most precious treasure
sitting with me like the purest gold
amidst my azure nostalgia.

"Electricity"

Lying with you is
the most exhilarating moment of my life.
Mushroom unfolding back
perfectly inside of itself.

When your lips meet mine
the feeling I get when being with you exceeds everything.

Watching electronic pixels.

Prism expanding as we are distracted by each other.

Please do not feel despondent.

No more guilt trips for the beautiful,
for your satisfaction fills me to the brim.

Your love encloses me with deep penetrating arrows
fresh from cupid's bow.

I am trying to perfect myself
to fulfill you as much as you fulfill me.
And, oh, how it thrills me.

You are my goddess,
my muse,
dancing on the tongue of solace,
concentrating with rushes of indecipherable feelings.

Feed me your fuel.

Hold me in your arms.

Never let go.

Stay with me, and as we awake at dawn,

we will feel the electricity once again.

"Object"

She sits silently smiling while stepping nearby,
willfully watching
where wonders are whirling in the wind,
blonde hair,
brown skin,
white teeth,
and piercing blue eyes.

Molded by surroundings, she's perfect;
now let's watch her descend.

A ceramic creation.

A porcelain portrait.

An earthenware object.

An ivory tower.

And for the duration, she internally hates it to be
a material subject in every hour.

"Remnant"

I open wide the smile of my memories.

This is to you:

I know we love each other the way we behave,
and I do not care who sees this message
written on the remnant of a lackadaisical evening.

All that matters is that it is true.

If I could explain my love for you
it would still be too pure for anyone
but ourselves to comprehend.

If my love was a beacon,
it would make the brightest star seem lonely.

"Enraptured"

Enraptured in your moment,

when I am lost in your beautiful eyes.

When I am with you my basic needs are useless.

You are all I have ever wanted,

and I cannot explain how happy that you are mine,

traveling in this enraptured moment.

I will take you to visit the celestial sphere,

and we might as well be the

only beings in existence

because nothing else is important.

"Rhythmic Echoes"

A beautiful rhythm of echoes

deep within my heart.

It rises like the flow and ebb of waves on a utopian shore.

In it lies the emotion of you and I in love,

wondrous and poetic.

This bond that we share, how it strengthens my heart from misery's stare

in this world of pain.

The only reward in life

is your smile that punctuates melancholy and despair.

Your hand embraces me from the strongest wind,

the deepest ocean, and the most sadistic society.

I want to shout to everyone

because you make me ecstatic.

My senses are construed.

My heart only feels.

I am so madly in love.

That is how I feel.

"Masterpiece"

Proportional goddess, you complete all abstracts,

forever coming as a beautiful release.

I have now beheld the new masterpiece;

the sun caught in your gilded hair.

Your complexion is entrancing.

Your heart is on fire and full of care and longing.

You are forever dancing in my mind.

I love to lie beside you,

alone with you and in your arms,

protecting me from life's dilemmas

and every aspect of harm.

"Incident"

I want to touch your face, and in that, touch the heavens.
I would like to be engulfed in your flames of bliss.

You make the superior bow to their knees.
The rays of the sun cannot hold you to their light.
You cannot be caged.
Your forest eyes are burning bright.

Let me reach for your silken skin.

You have me conquered, and I have fallen hard for you.
The golden hair of your blue-eyed beauty,
Well it has left me black and blue.

I long for you to mesmerize me,
and captivate me with your innocent touch.
Just know that since we have been,
of you I cannot seem to get enough.

You have me consumed,
and I cannot shake you from my thoughts,
and now as our lives lie in ruins,
I accept that it is all my fault.

"The Wilderness Within"

The wilderness within you sets my displacement aside.

Draw your delicate breath
as I bathe myself in your beauty.

I love it when you ignite
the fire inside that gleams so bright.

Your effervescing wonder
will camouflage my pain.
My ecstasy is with you
inside your gentle rain.
My mother tongue speaks
of things to be
and fights for the concept
of you and me.

"Prodigal Son"

As I lay dying places stones upon my chest,
so that I can go out doing what I do best,
being a thorn in the side of decency
in the face of sweet unrest.

Topple down my tower.
I need no lightning rod.
I'll simply drag my iron chair
in the midst of the thunderstorm
to sit and contemplate the reason I was born.

The gods saw you sunbathing and sent me off to war,
in hopes that I would get killed so that the angels
could come and collect you while I lie in the fields,
sweat in my hair and blood on my lips.

But I came staggering back like the prodigal son,
begging for one last chance for redemption.

"Cherubesque"

I remember one night,

the first time I looked at you.

Your image grabbed hold of me,

and it split my mind in two.

It left me there wanting more;

I just could not get enough,

of this feeling that you give to me,

I like to call it "love."

Explosive the atmosphere,

as we lie against each other's skin.

I want to love all that is you

and all that lies within.

I knew that you were beautiful;

I knew it from the start.

All of your romance performed a dance

that revitalized my heart.

Now that I know you more,

I never want to leave your side.

I only want to give to you

and let you never be denied

of the happiness that you deserve,

that I shall always give to you.

I'll make your every waking moment bliss

with all I say and do.

I like to wake up next to you
because I start off feeling strong,
but I could lie in bed and watch you
sleep all day long.
I'll stroke your hair and kiss your head,
and I'll hold your hand politely.
I'll lay my head upon your chest
and listen to you breathing lightly.

I still recall my butterflies
the first time that we met,
and you assured me, my dear,
that I've seen nothing yet.
You shined your light on top of me;
it was just what I needed.
It made me feel just like a god
who could not be defeated.

You rock my menial world
like no one has come close to.
So come to me, and stay with me
just like you're supposed to.
I can't believe I found you;
you're as perfect as can be.
I love everything about you
and all that you give to me.

Your smile is like a sunrise,
and your voice is so alluring,
and the time spent away from you

is all that is worth enduring.
Your body is smooth, your skin is soft;
it excites my tempted mind.
On bended knee, let passion flow
as we are intertwined.

Lying back, we perspire in passion
as we hold each other in revelry.
My body shakes, my mind it quakes
as we breathe together so heavily.
You fit perfectly into my arms,
so won't you stay the night?
Sleep with me my temptress,
hold me 'til the morning light.

My thoughts pour onto this paper
when I hold you in my head.
They could give me anything,
but I'd much rather have you instead.
Because in my mind you place inside
a quiet cherubesque elation.
While in my heart you seem to start
a gentle revelation.

"Sunlit Devotion"

You lie there with your strands of hair
lazily occupying your face,
the sunlight glinting off of your body.
You lay wrapped
in the mummification of yesterday's blaze,
awaiting for the perfect time to rise anew,
a modern goddess in an ancient race.

Give me glimpses so that I may take them
and continually sell them to myself throughout the
burning day and the hallowed night.
I grasp you, knowing that you emanate
the meaning of life.
I hold you in my gaze,
not wanting you to escape my finite line of vision.

Let me worship every inch of you.
Let me run my hands along your body.
Let me place my mouth unto your chalice
so that I may drink the elixir of life.
Let me enter your temple so that I may worship properly,
giving all of my ecstasy to you.

Let us lie in each other's reverence,
stroking each other, kissing each other.
Lie in my arms, like a puzzle piece fitting into place.
Let me kiss your head,

stroke your hair,

and wrap you in my arms

as we lie in the bliss that we have just created.

I will protect you while you rest.

Gaze with me into the sunrise,

to see what the coming day brings us.

Hold my hand as we amble through the fields.

Laugh with me, and show me your smile

as you skip and dance in your dress.

I watch as you move your body

while the sunlight shines through and you are glowing.

I want you to be mine forever and ever,

and I so desperately want to be yours.

"Eternal Embrace"

There is a venetian table in the corner
that holds the absolute weight of my heart.
The blood runs down in slow scarlet ribbons,
and it bleeds for you, my sweet counterpart.

The beat of a rhythmic procession
sounds marimbas in New Orleans' streets,
celebrating the renaissance of our love,
celebrating that I once again feel complete.

There is a sunset dripping colors like wax
against the sky, and they run down in streams.
I look to my left and see you breathing
amidst your slumber, your beauty, and dreams.

White smoke rises from burning tobacco
and swirls aimlessly into the night.
I sense embers within both of your eyes
while the flame within you I shall ignite.

In bed lies a lovely Greek goddess
carved out of marble, so smooth and so fair.
I lie down beside my statuesque princess;
I caress her body and play with her hair.

Now the moon is up high in the firmament.
It proudly boasts its artificial shine.
But even if the tides shift profoundly,
I am yours, and you shall forever be mine.

"Echoes of Blue"

The full moon looms nigh
through the coming of another day
As you read me your proclamation
and say what you have to say.
I listen on in silence
with a gaze that can't hide my mind.
I wish we could embrace like this
and leave it all behind.

Once you finished speaking,
you look to me in azure,
and in the moment,
I knew my love for you never was so sure.
I clung to you and you to me
as my tears slid down your breast
and then froze amidst the cold
that has grown between us.

The black phallic symbol around your neck
sways to and fro,
indecisive, like you and me,
not knowing which way to go.
We say nothing, but our eyes say it all,
laden with lover's dew.
Let me tremble in my weakness;
let me tremble next to you.

The blue world of faeries, lovers, and dreams
is always never what it seems.
Children lose their way at night
and lose their innocence in their sight,
but the blue world that is in your eyes
is always dressed in sweet surprise,
and the blue realm beneath your eyes
is charaded with no such disguise,
for the blue plane behind your eyes
holds utmost perfection I can surmise.

Underneath the sky of blue
that is in your vibrant eyes,
I saw mysteries of life dancing
'neath that very same sky.

Stop my slipping.
Call my bluff.
Pin me against the wall,
with your stare and your stony smirk.
Catch me when I fall.
Create with me a sheer disposition,
and solicit, from me, belief.
Move my mind to vulnerable positions,
and bring my racing heart relief.

Your indivisible primary faculties,
your undying sentiments
enhance the minute subtleties
of your lovely innocence.
If I come on too strong,
grab me and let me know,
for I feel that I have known you
a lifetime ago.

I writhe inside the sun
trying to find warmth once again
because my love is frozen on the ground
much to my chagrin.
I twist beyond the moon
searching for stars up in the sky,
but when I reach the brightest one,
I realize it has long since died.

Take away this drunken cup
that's worn down at the rim.
Give me all your electric light,
for my vision is growing dim.
We are both so damaged from our past,
from the heartache and the loss.
We are willing to try anything
that is lined with gold and frost.

I tried to be a perfect man,
but I could not run the race,
so now a funeral for love is in the mirror,
staring at my face.

You cover up your faults with ammunition,
and wrap your wounds with gauze,
and you give a gift to any person
who will give you his applause.

I want to follow you to where you will lay waiting
amidst the alabaster and the stone.
It's frightening from all the lightning,
and I do not want to be alone.

I took in all of your blackness,
as it lingered in your glass.
I asked if it was catching,
but you said to let it pass.
My future is bleak; my present is unpleasant.
I don't know what to do.
I thought, like you, I could live in the past,
but the blackness got that too.
I used to love the bright days
and the beauty all around,
but now I have caught your blackness,
and its weight pulls me down.

I let the landslide swallow me
and extinguish my very soul.
I am not the monster that you have seen;
I am simply in a hole.
You long to fix those around you,
to make them long for your gold.
You try to clothe and feed me,
but I am neither starved nor cold.
I now long for you always,
without want and without need.
It is merely an instinct
that is not driven by some greed.
You say you want to part from me
to give you some relief,
but now, my dear, I can feel you
when you cry and breathe.

The silverware grows dull,
in the dim light of the café,
a specter sits at my table,
in a lover's sheer array.
It whispers of lost chances,
and paths we didn't stay,
but I hurl my pride into the void,
and grasp the wilted bouquet
I wanted to be everything for you,
to sing you every song.
Did my words bring you comfort?

No, I sang the lyrics wrong.
I spent my life for you,
through every fiber and every trace.
I was granted wishes,
but all I wished for was your embrace.

I long to hold you my dear,
even though our love is far away.
I know it will not come tomorrow,
because it is not here today.
It's as though you were a masterpiece
in some European town,
where the pilgrims come to worship
and the priests all write you down,
but I still long to hold you tonight
as we finally admit defeat
because for the past three weeks,
skeletons have danced beneath my feet.

"Hollow Dissonance"

I scream
until my vocal chords
are ripped
from my thrapple;
the screams reverberate against the walls
and vibrate in the arms of people
who claim they understand,
yet I can't help but feel like yesterday's man.

The tide changes in unexpected ways,
and everyone turns with the rays of the moon,
but when I start to lose control,
I am crucified like the oh-so-hated Christ figure
of your wildest repulsion.

You seem to wait for Abel
while you seem to wait for Cain,
but you choose the one who finds you
when you hear what you only want to hear.

You find yourself in a senseless war
while I am merely trying to explain why I am doing what I do,
but that does not match up with your schema
of the way things are supposed to be.

You say I had a household of love and understanding,
but you don't know the other half,
the half that told me not to cry,
the half that told me not to bleed,
the half that told me not to run to people's arms
when in my hour of need.

I lived in a false Babylon,
and the hanging gardens were my
desired nooses
that I wished would wrap their tendrils
around my neck,
until I would feel no more.

Pointed are your words, so let me be pointed in mine,
if only for a moment.
You don't know what you have until it disappears;
you never had it.

You never had the warmth I had,
only to have it ripped away from your very existence.

Can I not sit in myself?
Just because you are unable to do so,
is it so abhorrent
that I may want to merely sit and ponder
amidst the day's dying sun?

You hurl at me unreasonable responses
that are immature and heated,
without thought,
without pragmatism.

You understand the Judas
whom has betrayed you time and time again
for his 20 pieces of silver,
but you do not understand Pilate's notion
of doing what he has to do despite the backlash,
the anguish,
the remorse of reacting in a way that is only natural
and oh so human.
Allow me to witness your exquisite essence unveiled,
as you would tenderly reveal it to a cherished soul.

The remnants of love that you offer me,
are the remnants that I have left behind.
Your pain and past is no credential here;
it's just the shadow of my soul.

In realms devoid of solace, where emptiness wears thin,
what echoes fill the spaces where your journey's been?
You confide your lover's plight, a limb in fracture grim,
restless whispers linger, his presence casts a dim.
I glimpsed the man you mention, just the other night,
feasting on a lady where shadows merge with light.

Oh, solace flees from covens
where the witches hold their sway,
And a cunning doctor's hand
did cleanse her womb away.
The man of fervent spirit
is the revolution's guide,
and he taught scores of women
how to halt an unborn tide.

You have shouldered your acceptance
like a gun you can never hope to aim.
Where are you?
Where are you?

Where tread the heroes in their fame?
I ponder aloud as the veil starts to fray
Did I merely limp?
Was I truly tame?

"Soul Attention"

I watch the excitement of each day
surely go a'passin'.
I see the fantasies that you might have
and the pain is still surpassing
all rational thoughts I have,
for there's still the fear you want someone else,
and if this is the utmost case,
then relieve me of this Hell.

I am yours and yours is mine.
I thought I'd made that clear?
It's nice to have innuendos,
but what good are they without us here?
I want your eyes to look to me,
to me and to no one else.
I may be totally selfish,
but I love you and myself,

together as two are meant to be
and meant to be for the end of time.
So don't let your eyes or mind wander,
for I am here to match your rhyme.
I dare you to find anyone
with as much zeal, and zest, and kink.
I dare you to find another one
who can hear your thoughts when you sit and think.

I know I don't have all material pleasures
to bestow upon you now,
but if you would just give me your sole attention
then I will make it worthwhile somehow.
So stare at me in words of grandeur,
and fantasize only about me.
And I will give you all the love you want,
and I will give you the affection you need.

"Full Circle"

Oh Darling, oh my dearest one,
we have come full circle again.
You have shared our bouts of foolishness
much to my chagrin.
Your cries I hear, and me, you fear,
but our hearts continue beating.
What does not kill us makes us stronger,
our demons are retreating.
But pain, anguish, desolation,
the crimson ribbons are unfolding
from our beaten souls and bodies
from this past that we have been holding.

Oh Darling, oh my dearest one,
ascend and feel my love,
for it is enough to make the angels jealous
that reside up above.
A sharp wit and a common dismay
that resides within our minds
is enough to look the other way
and leave the other one behind.
But lover, my wondrous friend,
rest your head upon my arm.
I never want to bring you pain
or let you experience any harm.

My darling lies asleep,
her body twisted in its knots,
while I am awake, and with her freckles,
I play connect-the-dots.
I promise you that you are safe
as long as you are with me.
For without you I am lost
and searching restlessly.
I call your name and rejoice in you
the love that you have brought.
For the idea of us not together
leaves me so distraught.

"Tempest of the Murky Waters"

At times, I long for the sea to take me too.
It was blind clairvoyance that drew me to you.
You were a phenomenon of poignancy like a thousand
widowed ravens screaming at the moon.

Life is a river, and at times we yearn for the bottom,
as a way to measure the way things change.
We are caught in the eye of a gradual storm,
counting the years.
I know it seems dark and the frost comes,
but it comes through the very cracks that
let the happiness through.

Blame me for any disaster, and I will
forever be your martyr.
I will not let the kerosene run dry
where we make our beds in familiar cemeteries
between the longing for death and the searching for life.

Let us crawl through the canyons
and swim amidst the mire,
rusty chains and leaden coats.
We will be fatigued and jaded,
but at least we will not be chasing some endless nothing
down the metaphorical rabbit hole.
Let us stand on the ledge of optimism
you with a feather, me with a parasol.
Slouch in the darkness.
Hang off of barstools and seedy environments.
We traded war stories.
We knew we could trust each other,
so we both let each other listen.

You may think you have it all figured out,
what will bring you satisfaction,
but you would just be starting a journey in
a broken-down car.

Run if you want to,
but time is the ballast,
change is a constant,
and emotion is a trigger.
You can run if you want to,

But soon enough the rain and despair
will slide right in like a brooding lullaby.

Saddle up for the bacchanal ride.
Bring the celebration to your soul.
I have got a cup full of whiskey,
so bring your broken radio.

There are lines on your forehead
from trying to thread the needle of your
idea of perfection without telling me.
If you allow me, I will throw the atlases
out of the window,
and we can take the longest way home.

Sometimes it seems I never won you over
but merely caught you on a good day.
Sometimes you feel like the best lover
that I am not allowed to love.

I too once experienced the cold steel to my temple,
the razor to my skin,
and I too was once lost in a world that
rocks back and forth like a catamaran
lost amid a tempest at sea.

In whispers woven, we find our voice unheard,
silent symphony, where words never stirred.
Amidst the garden of roses, we're forget-me-nots,
in shadows cast, our light fiercely sought.

Like flashlights in the darkest night's embrace,
we trace constellations, seeking solace in space.
Connecting dots in cosmic dance's trance,
seeking sense in the celestial expanse.

Our fingerprints are sore from thumbing through pages,
looking for some escape,
but all the capital letters convey the same thing…
there is no escape from ourselves.

Do not compromise between remembering
and learning how to forget
because a simple act like taking in light
is now like trying to move boulders with your breath.

So when will the signs stop pointing to an idealized
version of what life is supposed to be?
When will our thoughts stop drifting like vapor
over the path where we used to walk?

I created a room for you up near the heavens,
so let us not hold that place
dog-eared and forgotten anymore.
All the over-encrypted poetry and prose,
unintelligible stories of truth
were all soaked in enigma.
So let's drop the metaphors and symbolism.
Let us both come clean.
Our attempts to be forthright are illusory to the point
that we do not even know it.
Our life is a story of burning bridges,
allowing time to pass,
forgiveness, and breaking things with our hands.
Life is a story of loaded glances
and leaning in too far.

Some delusions are never meant to be realized.
Some regrets can be prevented by reading
the writing on the wall.

We are children, returning to responsibility
with the smell of campfire smoke on our clothes.
Suicidal sunrise and tears upon our faces are stalled
by fantasies and patterns that assure us
will make us feel better,
but they are hollow promises.

You know me pretty well,
but I would bargain with the devil
just to keep you.
I used to not let you see my dark side,
so now I scream down the freeway
at the top of my lungs
praying for the strength to do something reckless.

I swear I am not cynical.
I am still just bitter
at the people who murdered my love songs
mid-verse...people just like you.

I get it.

You have been building these walls
all of your life,
but I ask that you let me help
deconstruct them
before you flash me another smile
while you lay another stone.

Instead of building a wall,
help me build a guardrail that will keep us both from
falling off this ledge once more.

"Portrait of Ambition"

She sits and gazes at artificial prisms and pixels,
determined to reach the next rung
of the proverbial ladder
like Icarus,
striving to attain the warmth and security of the sun.

Her fingers tap like that of a postmodernist
who has just finished her second condensated scotch,
but the scotch is now gone,
and the ice clinks against the insides
of the now barren glass.

Her long statuesque legs are crossed over one another
as she sits and contemplates the theories of Euclid.
The mannerisms of frustration are painful
yet adoring to watch:
her brow furrows,
her hand meets her mouth and curls around her jaw
as if she is trying to pry the correct words
from her mouth that are so close
yet so far out of reach.

She then reaches for her book,
scribbling in importance here and there,
marking her accomplishments and goals.
She has done it!
She has completed the first stage of her dream.

And as she leans over to put her belongings into her bag,
her breasts spill into view, pouring out of her blouse,
longing for my lips and tongue to caress them.

Perhaps I can lure her into the darkened bedroom
and watch her delicate feet move across the linoleum floor,
like precise,
calculated,
premeditated pirouettes of a ballerina.

She frustrates me, but I love her all the same.

"Symphony of the Night"

The moon has waned to crescent.
My despair has waxed to bliss.
I love to be in your presence,
when you hold me and when we kiss.

I love every little thing about you,
your mannerisms and your quips,
and I love to sing about you,
for you exist in books and scripts.

Your kisses are like windows;
they let the sunshine in.
Your hugs are like a willow
that hold me steady when I spin.

My heart is made of strings
that strum poetry and songs for you,
about all the little things
that made me fall in love with you.

They bend and twist and vibrate
for all you say and do.
I hope their mark is not missed,
for I want you to feel it too

"An Anatomical Quest"

Anatomy of the epitome of female,
smooth highlands and ivory loins.
You are the earth in your philosophy of giving,
providing, and being maternal.
My unworthy and provincial body
yearns to cultivate you,
so much that the sun will swell and deluge
from the extent of our world.

I walked solitary as a chasm
in which life vanished from my gaze.
I was ravaged by the striking,
bittersweet allure of the night.
To endure my loneliness,
I forged you like a shining rapier,
like a bullet in my gun,
like an H-Bomb in slow reverse.

But the moment of assent rings out,
and I love you.

Body,
hair,
movements like dances,
laughter like Spring dew landing on the grass.

I shall drink from the vessel of your breasts,
and gaze into the worlds that are your eyes.
I shall inhale and taste the flowers of your private places
where no one but me is allowed to trespass.

Anatomy of my lady,
I will persevere in your delicacy.
My appetite for you is a relentless
and ardent quest.
The quest is made of dark and mysterious mountaintops,
where my eternal thirst follows you
into the depths of night.

"The Radiant Apology"

I am regretful that the overwhelming day-to-day
has caused me to lash out at you.
You, full of light and of royal musings.
You do not deserve such backlash.
I fear I am resorting to old ways.
I do not want to repress.
The fact of the matter is I feel I am drowning.
You are inestimable.
Each night before I drift off,
I long to count your fingers and toes,
to feel the rhythmic procession of your heart,
to see your chest rise and fall, over and over again,
to ensure you are still with me.

You are good enough.
You are more than good enough.
You are absolutely wonderful.
At the end of the day, you bring me joy
in more ways that are possible to count:
A smile springs to my bitter face as I rub
and scratch the top of your head,
making your mane move back and forth
atop your pretty crown.
To land my lips on a full cheek
is my way of exalting the gods.
To rub your feet, caress your legs,
and stroke the tops of your hands are the ways
in which I pray and find solace
in an otherwise dark world.
You have been there for me,
and I fear of driving you away.

You see, you have done nothing wrong,
for I am the one who drags his iron chair,
to sit in, in the midst of a thunderstorm.
I love you, my dear, until my heart beats its last beat,
and until my lungs fill with air for the very last time.

"Simpatico Reverie"

I feel as if the being within you and the being within me
are
inextricably
intertwined.

The light,
the gibbous,
within our connected being
will never dim, making the artificial incandescence
of the world seem hollow and burnt out,
as if it were never shining at all.

When we doff our garments to the floor below,
and lie, bare, next to each other,
I love how our legs are like the vines of ivy swirling,
reticulating,
and gripping each other amidst the alluvial plane.

When I awake, I like to burnish away the thoughts
produced by sleep that have become published
amongst the interlaced linens of our love-making.

I want to lie down with you
and escape into the astute and somber musings of the eve.
The technicolor depravity
that the unknown of tomorrow holds
fills me with dread and feels like another's experience
and not mine,
but then I turn my gaze to you
and see you in your repose,
you and your grace affirm,
upon my face,
a perpetual rictus.

When you sleep, the consistency of your breathing
reminds me that I am alive.

And while the thoughts linger in my head
like black and savage stars in an unholy night,
our simpatico reminds me what it means to truly love
and feel loved.

"Nothing in Between"

Love is arduous.
Love is kind.
Love forgives all the momentary lapses of reason
that reside dormant within ourselves
until the worst time for them to break free,
into a clouded night, arrives.

My love for you is written all around us.
My love for you resonates
until the voice does not have strength
to give a soft reply, yet it replies anyway;
it replies amidst the struggles and studies
of battle
and
war,
the perfect storm that builds up inside of us all.

My love for you burns on an eternal wick,
not giving or yielding to the Northern winds,
the zephyrs,
or tempests
that toss ships aside at sea.

Let me fall asleep with my arm around you,
with your feet twitching against mine,
with your breath so perfectly in sync with mine
that we are but one being.
Let me lull you to sleep with goodness
and pure unadulterated love.
Your love for me is like a gut-wrenching
chalice of essence
that no other person could ever hope to equate to.

Each morning when I awake,
my first springing and infantile thought is
"What can I do for her?
"What can I do for her on a day such as today?"
For, you see, I awake, thinking of you.
I work, longing for you.
I relax, yearning for you.
I shower, thirsting for you.
And I sleep, dreaming of you.

I dream of the alabaster finish upon your skin.
I long for the feel of your body against mine.
I thirst for your lips,
your kiss,
your embrace,
your everything.

Nothing can quench or satiate the need that I carry for you
each
and
every
day
of my waking life.

You have lit the flame of reason within me.
You have inspired the breath of life inside my soul.
You have placed a smile on a face,
A laughter in my heart,
and a light that will not be extinguished
by any mortal or immortal force.

I am merely an evidence of life,
and if your life is burning
well then, I am simply the ash.
And if you ever decide to go your way,
then I will go your way too.
For I did not choose to fall in love
because it is never up to you,
but you were walking in my mind,
and I was passing through.

Lay your worries aside, and lay with me instead.
Put the past where it is...the past, behind you.
Look forward to the coming days with me.
Because I will worship, adulate, and exalt all that is you,
unlike anything you have ever hoped to feel before.

If I am your magician then you are,
without doubt,
the magic.
I am yours.
You are mine,
and there is nothing in between.

"Whispers in the Clouds"

Fly off with me into the cumulus, kissing the clouds
while we wait for the rain to christen our bodies.

There was a shape of a sinister thought,
but you protected me.

I may not always say it,
or act in the grand scheme of things,
but I love you.
I love your independence.
I love your free-thinking trampoline of love
that I can never get off of.

When I first met you,
I heard the building cacophony of my past
deteriorating,
crumbling.
And when the smoke cleared
and the debris scattered,
I heard the tone of the bell in my ears
when the quiet came.

I regret at times that I am the rust on the gears…
Trigger happy, straight jacket,
holding onto my patterns
and my liquid medication.

You taught me breathing lessons,
and I gave to you bleeding poems
that were stuck in the bottom of my throat
for my entire life...
no one had come along to release them yet,
to set them free, no one until you.

Please do not discard me or run for the coast,
for my chest will be howling
with the songs of your ghost.

Keep my heartbeat between your thumb and forefinger,
under your pillow while you lie asleep.

When you and I are apart
I feel you in my stomach while you are living,

Through my mind you drop thoughts down
telepathically
and they roll around my insides.

Let me be penitent and kneel from time to time,
and let me be hurt and in anguish.
Take me back for I am the remnants
of a person who almost did not get away.

You are the bow in the lace that ties me to splendor.
You are the precious metal in the river of my veins.
You are the forward progress to throw my shutters open,
and you are the light before the day.

I keep thinking of the night when all the lights went out
and how you taught me to see in the dark.

Remind me how to be brave, because I have forgotten.
I have forgotten where blood sweat and tears go
when they're tired and spent,
because after the wreckage the scared person in me
crawled back to the shelter,
the shelter of your arms,
your chest,
and your beating heart.

"Soundly Sleeping"

To see you lie there soundly sleeping
is what makes my heart start leaping.
You are the one I want to be keeping.
What you sow I shall be reaping
to nurture all my senses sweeping
me off of my feet.

I lay on you and I am feeding
on your essence that keeps me needing
all your love that is exceeding
as the sweat on my brow is beading.
Never shall I be misleading,
for I'm ecstatic that we accrete.

Your movements cause me to become beguiling,
as I watch you sweetly smiling.
The love for you I am compiling
into a thought that's reconciling.
Your life path number I am dialing
because you are oh so sweet.

I look at you and start to wonder
how you took my fears and torn them asunder.
Your gaze makes my heart to thunder.
I want to give you all my plunder,
and never make you feel a blunder.
I am the swamp and you are my peat.

"At a Loss"

I could not rise from my bed
nor answer the telephone.
I was sinking into the trenches;
I was cold and all alone.
I sank and settled in the darkest mire,
just me and my soul.
I was searching for the inevitable trash
that I paid for in full.

And the winter of your discontent
started long before you met me.
You were too damaged to think,
and you were much too blind to see.
I simply sat and watched you two
from a separated empty street
as my instinct looked to me
and returned my smile of defeat.

I moved on with the blowing winds,
or at least I told myself so,
but in reality, even though you hurt me,
I did not want you to go.
I tried to learn from you what I could,
and for you I tried to teach,
but the only fact that I learned
was that you were in another person's reach.

I know I may not ever be the one to you
who has got away,
but in the future, you will love me more,
this I shall always pray.
Please do not put me in his shadow,
not once more nor ever again.
Do not make me feel second-rate
like some neglected used best friend.

I always tried to make you feel loved
with my poetry and my art.
I was simply preparing my depression
for when you stabbed me in the heart.

One,
two,

three women,
I have driven into the arms of another man.

I know I have my faults,
but I suppose I was just not better than…

…someone who abandoned you
and your creation in an hour of need,
someone who neglected you,
someone who made you cry and bleed.
I suppose my little flame it failed,
but at least, in you, I ignited a spark.
I wanted to be your Charlemagne
while you would be my Joan of Arc.

I praised your face and your eyes;
I praised your body and your hair.
I praised the way you traipsed around
in your T-Shirt and no underwear.
I threw my passions to the wind
and immersed myself in this war,
but in the end it seemed I had lost,
for you seemed to love him more.

You clung to false nostalgia
while the present was staring you in the face.
You did not want to confront the mirror;
you preferred his chains to my embrace.
There was a mist of sweet swirling kisses
as we lit up each other's dark.
Our rivalry was vicious,
but his dominion over you was still at large.

They all say that I should have seen it coming,
that I would have a broken heart.
Yes, we were an impressive couple,
but I feel I merely played a minor part.
I have pored over my perseverance;
it has been dirtied up and scarred,
for my dignity is like a porpoise,
and my insecurity is like a shark.

My confidence has been oh so bruised,
now the third time is the charm.
I only want to give you all I can,
so your past I can sever and disarm.

I just want to be loved by you,
much stronger than you have ever loved him,
but if you ever view his grass as greener,
then I will not be able to do this ever again.
And there is nothing left in this world
that I wish to ever say or do
except to sit in my agony
and despair
and uncertainty
and wonder
if you
are as tired as I am of running away
from love and simply leaving,
for the pattern that I seem to be stuck in
has me altruistically believing

that we are joined at the spirit,
and we are conjoined in the mind.
We are joined in our anxiety
and panic as we have both been so maligned.
There is a lilac in your hair,
and there is a dead carnation in my trust.
I feel the ship is sinking
as the sea of your past turns my boat to rust.

You talk of his past lovers,
and you talk of him in nonchalance,
but you should view him as a sunset,
and you should view me as the dawn.
You send pictures of him to me, on accident,
and to whomever else,
but if this is the life we are forced to live
then I will excuse me of this Hell.

It feels like you are still pining after him;
it feels like we are living with his ghost,
but when you call me by his name
are the moments that hurt me the most.
I sit and wonder if, at times,
I feel like you felt with the one he met before you,
but it does not matter now anyways
because you need to wish your past adieu.

I am out of my ever-loving mind,
and I am out of my self-destructive head.
If I must choose between death

and you still loving him, I will rather end up dead.
I know I may not ever hope to be
the same as your one who did get away,
but I am the one who is here right now,
to love you each and every day.

"The Bearing of Historical Weight"

Now let us just lie in the beds that our upbringing made.

Hold my heart in your teeth,
for if I cannot be your love then what will I be?

Memories and repressions hold like an anchor
through the pain and the blood, and we drag it behind.

I know my inadequacies and insecurities
get the best of me from time to time,
but I have been here before,
and sometimes I still cannot talk myself down.
I see the view from the catacombs.

I needed strong hands to pull me over the hill
before I loved you again,
because the feeling was that of a ship that was sinking,
and the load was an eminence of antiquated suffering.

Your rose retreated yet came blooming again,
but the ground was my heart slowly breaking.
It is him or it is me said my love to your sour memory

"Love's Dignitary"

The love and gratitude and appreciation
that I hold for you has a regular recurrence
in a way that is so ceremonious,
that the sages and oracles of yore
are at a loss of words themselves.

From your gentle acclivity
protrudes a Seraphic piece of heart
that keeps keen poignant agonies at bay.

Your beauty is a dignitary
that should be embraced
with perfect manifestations of reverence
and forms of obeisance.

"The Essence of a Whisper"

I love to lie with you
and stroke your skin so fair.
I love to kiss you up and down
while tousling your silken hair.
The way you smile at me
makes me forget the reality I'm in.
The way your eyes sparkle,
make my light ignite within.

You are the fire in my loins.
The sin within my soul.
You are the one who makes me feel deconstructed,
while at the same time makes me whole.

Your laugh and your touch
make me feel like I'm up above.
The little things about you,
are the things in which I love.

I could write a million pages
and one thousand words that rhyme,
but all the notebooks I could fill
could never describe our time
that is spent in throes together,
that is spent in each other's arms.
I want to protect you from all of humanity
and from all of the world's harm.

I run my fingers across your feet
and across your silken skin.
Like I have already stated,
you are my soul; you are my sin.

The light and life that shoots from your eyes
are more than I could ever need.
They give me feelings I cannot describe,
for I adore you so much indeed.

The laugh that escapes your mouth
is like the chiming of a bell.
Your smile is like medicine
that keeps me feeling well.

So come into my presence.
Make me full with all your ways.
Perplex me with your touch.
Hypnotize me with you gaze.

I want to make you feel enlightened
as often as I can.
You are the prettiest incarnation
in the form of mortal woman.

"My Painted Lady"

Your countenance is so alluring,
and the love we have is reassuring
through the trials and tribulations
of existence as a whole.
And when I gaze upon you sleeping,
my love for you, I am keeping
keeping in a shadow box
so that I might share with you, my soul.
Keeping in a locked container
that is as sacred as the scrolls.
You are the ember; I am the coal.

And perspicaciously I remember
that in the cold November
is when I gazed upon the Seraphim
that resides above the sky.
I look to you when I am hurting
and when life seems disconcerting,
and the only happiness that I have
is when with you I lie.
And the only bliss I get from life
is from you who gets me by.
You are more beautiful than Versailles.

The way you dance in the rhythm
of a perfect algorithm
makes me want to throw away
all I knew and all I will know.
You make my heart take rapid beating,
and still I stand, and still repeating
that I will do anything for you
until life deals me the death blow.
I will do my best for you
like a ravenous rainbow.
I am the starry night,
and you are my Van Gogh.

You made the boy in me grow stronger;
I wish to placate you much longer
than you have ever had the pleasure
of knowing what that means.
You take my smile and make it wider,
no longer am I an outsider

but a servant who will worship you
through all the in-between.
I will dedicate myself to you,
through the great and the obscene.
You surround my soul like gabardine.

We made love in the soft clearing,
and there were tears throughout your peering,
that gave your eyes, so deep and blue,
an iridescent shine.
The words of us were left unspoken,
but solid as the redwoods, oaken,
they knew our bond would be left unbroken
through spirits intertwined.
Our love and body and soul and brain
are more potent than strychnine.
I am yours, and you are mine.

My faculties were slow returning,
as the light from you, it kept me burning,
burning through the hollow night
and through the lonely bitter cold.
I thought you were a dream come true,
but the dream has since bid adieu
and has turned into reality,
yet my urges cannot be controlled.
My lust and desire and want for you pushes
against the strong threshold.
The ways I am aroused are manifold.

I open up your bedroom door
and see you kneeling on the floor,
ready to take me in your mouth
while I hold your pretty head.
You choke upon my phallic rod,
while praying to a Pagan god.
Your Pagan god could give me the world,
but I'd rather have you instead.
I would rather worship that which is in front of me
than feeling so misled.
You are my personal figurehead.

And since we have been reconciling,
you've put my state into smiling,
smiling for the person you are,
and who you inspire me to be.

I stroke your body and lick your chalice
while watching aurora borealis
in your eyes and in your head;
I've found gold within the debris.
You are the elite, the epitome of all,
amidst a field of bourgeoisie.
I am you, and you are me.

So stay with me don't keep me guessing,
for you my love I am expressing
all the things you do for me
that make me feel like a better man.
Lay your head upon my shoulder;
stay with me while we grow older.
Before I laid my eyes on you I thought
"My life has not began."
I life had not been lived at all
until you helped me understand.
Your simplest wish is my command.

"My Painted Lady: Redux"

It's an idle existence oil paint
of a far-gone afternoon,
as the moonbeams break through the curtains
and flickerings bathe the room.

We sit and sip the coffee
that we made in the early morn,
as feelings of indifference
were slowly but surely born.

We both want to explore the soul
of each other, day by day.
We both yearn to tell our troubles
yet can't find the right words to say.

I know you are depressed
and dissociative now and then,
but you must know that I will love you
through dark time and time again.

You know that I am depressed
and repressed with such strong doubt,
but the feelings of you, good or bad,
are the feelings I cannot live without.

You can read your zodiac mystics
while I read my Robert Frost,
and we can note our place with bookmarks,
the momentum that we have lost.

My phone is off the hook,
I only wish yours was the same.
Because I long to talk and laugh with you,
and I long to scream your name.

And the seas are blue,

as blue as your eyes,
and I shall take them with me
when I go off to die.

And if I write you words by the sun,
please read them by the moon,
for they seem to glow better at nighttime
than they do in the afternoon.

Your smile is a 40-watt bulb
that lights the essence I have seen.
And your presence is that of angels,
the likes I have never seen.

So come with me, and only me,
let me be your only one.
For you have loved others in the past,
but that is gone now that we are one.

"Dance of Uncertainty"

Thanks for the dance
So short and so sweet,
Maybe some other day
I can make your heart skip a beat
Like all the other beautiful people
That you see on the street.

Thanks for the dance
One, two three, three, two, one.
I was so us,
And you were so one.
Should I apologize
For not being so weirdfully beautiful
Or so beautifully weird?
You must escape me,
And it is just as I feared.

But you're the only one
Who can feel lonely and blue,
Yet when I feel this way
You turn to the you
That is young and bored
With the stagnancy you've found,
Yet you do nothing about it
Except sit and be drowned.

I know I'm not perfect or strikingly fierce
I just want to take your heart
With my love and then pierce
The love in you that is absent.

I found flowers in your hair,
And your spirit is bare
We've been wearing our costumes forever.
So turn up our music,
And pour out the wine,
And stop at my surface,
For I feel my surface is fine.

And if the gods weren't so crazy
And did not want us to love one another
Then why did they make our bodies so sweet?

Sometimes I feel lonely, I don't know what to do.
I'd trade all my sorrow for a fresh hit of you.
I want us to be eternal, tomorrow wouldn't be soon,
So I'll tell you my plans of a counterfeit moon.

There are days I need escape you as well,
And there are days I see others
But I want to be with you
Because you are so worth it.

I do not share what is ours
Whether it is the good or the bad,
For it is ours and no one else's
To see what the damage we've had.

I've stepped into a chaotic world,
And it's covered up my heart.
I am not this deformity that you see.
I am not one you should tear apart.

You strike my side with carelessness
As you search for your happiness.
The helpless one you see before you
Does not long for your thirstiness.
I do not ask for your validation
Or the center of your world.

When I am on top of the world
You do not raise me there
Your longings do not oblige me
To lay myself naked and bare.
I myself am the pedestal
For this ugliness at which you stare.

If you wish to preside over my pain
You must find out what makes me nice
The remnants of your love that you offer me
Are merely pieces of jagged ice.
Your past is no credential here,
It's just the silhouette of my wounds.

I longed for you since the beginning,
But you have longed for a world that's not mine.
I have put everything out for you,
But you have others waiting in line.
You say you must escape from me,

Yet I can hear you when you breathe.
Do not dress in ragged cloths for me,
For I know you are not that poor.
And don't say you love me unconditionally
When you yourself are not sure.
It is your turn to prove yourself,
For it is your flesh I have begun to wear.

Printed in Great Britain
by Amazon